FORMBY

THEN & NOW

IN COLOUR

REG & BARBARA YORKE

This book is a somewhat late contribution to 'Civic Day',
organised by the Formby Civic Society, June 2012.

First published in 2012

The History Press
The Mill, Brimscombe Port
Stroud, Gloucestershire, GL5 2QG
www.thehistorypress.co.uk

ISBN 978 0 7524 7155 6

Typesetting and origination by The History Press
Printed in India.

CONTENTS

ACKNOWLEDGEMENTS

We are very pleased to have this opportunity to celebrate the half century of local history research and recording that has accelerated since the Formby Civic Society came into being in 1953. In our attempt to show a little of how Formby has changed (and is still changing), we are very grateful once again to the founder members of the society for recording Formby as it was when the society was founded, and for assembling an extensive archive of historical photographs.

Whilst the role of Muriel Sibley is very well remembered and the society still possesses a treasure trove of her work, both photographic and artistic, the efforts of others, not only the founder members but those who have followed and are still active today, deserve our thanks.

During the last decade or so we have tried to add to the pool of knowledge about the history of our community. And in this we have been helped by new and active members of the society and others with a professional interest in the past, present and future – not only of Formby but of the whole Sefton Coast.

One current member, Tony Bonney, has in particular been of immense help during recent years in digitally copying not only most of the Sibley collection but also a large part of our extensive newspaper-cutting archive. These he has also digitally indexed for ease of access. In the last few months he has followed up this good work by adding to our photographic record by taking many of the 'present-day' photographs reproduced in this publication.

Barbara and I are responsible for the text and for any mistakes or misinterpretations. Please let us know if you spot any errors. Finally, we would like to thank: the many people who have provided information and/or photographs, particularly Sefton Coast & Countryside for the photograph of Wicks Lane Lake (page sixty); Major Bill Hunter for the photograph of Altcar Rifle Range (page seventy); Phil and Muriel Clulee for the photograph of Wilson's Garage (page seventy-seven); the publishers for inviting us to undertake this work; and the Formby Civic Society again for its support. We have enjoyed compiling this book and hope that our readers will enjoy our efforts.

ABOUT THE AUTHORS

Since Reg Yorke's retirement from his medical career, and Barbara Yorke's from her work as a magistrate (for which she was delighted to receive an MBE), the authors have continued in their joint enjoyment of local history. Their original research resulted in the remarkable discovery that Formby lifeboat station, established by 1776, was not only Britain's first such station but also the world's first. They have been writing about local history since the early 1980s but still enjoy discovering interesting new things about the area they have lived in for over half a century.

INTRODUCTION

Formby is a compact town. Its shopping centre – still referred to affectionately by its inhabitants as 'the village' – is situated approximately 10 miles north of Liverpool. Probably in existence even prior to Norse settlement, growth and expansion began in 1848 when the railway from Liverpool to Southport was opened, making Formby more accessible. Until then, Formby had been a small rural hamlet. By 1900 the population had doubled to 5,000, and by 1905 the area won Urban District Council status. By the mid-1950s Formby's population had doubled once again to some 10,000 inhabitants. Serious expansion continued after 1959 when a start was made on several large housing estates. The population is now approximately 25,000, including Little Altcar.

Nevertheless, local government now anticipates allowing the building of thirty-six new dwellings per year for the next fifteen years. Attempts are being made to identify suitable sites. However, if this is done there is bound to be considerable impact. This is all the more reason to document photographically some of the changes we have witnessed in the last century.

Geographically, Formby can be considered a virtual 'island' in the green belt, bounded by the sea to the west and farmland to the east; by RAF Woodvale to the north and 620 acres occupied by Altcar Rifle Range to the south. The sandy coastal strip has high protection for its wildlife, being designated as a Site of Special Scientific Interest and a Special Area of Conservation, and includes two National Nature Reserves.

During the last decade we have been privileged to contribute to various aspects of coastal history. Our joint research began with establishing the history of Formby Lifeboat Station. We are now gratified that an eminent Canadian maritime historian agrees with our proposition that Formby's station was, in fact, the first in the world. We are not likely to be able to make a similar claim ever again, but are participating fully in the Sefton Coast Partnership's research into the history of the coast, particularly as it relates to Ravenmeols – the 'twice lost settlement'. We are delighted to find that others are keen to assist with this and look forward to jointly discovering much more about the past of the place where we have lived for nearly sixty years.

In the present volume we have looked at past images of Formby and Ravenmeols, and made comparison with the same buildings or location today. This process has highlighted how fast this area is changing – but perhaps we might have made the same comment had we been doing this study a century ago. This does, however, underline the importance of having a record, both pictorial and descriptive. We hope the present attempt, as partial as it is, will be looked at with interest long after we have gone.

Reg and Barbara Yorke, 2012

THE 'VILLAGE'

THE CORNER OF Three Tuns Lane in around 1900. The street lamp on the left was Formby's first experiment with street lighting, using acetylene gas. The policeman is Inspector Fyfe, and Mr Birtwistle, the grocer, is the man wearing the white coat. Also visible is Mr Hayworth, a draper. Some of the property on Chapel Lane was still private housing and some shops had rather nice verandas until the mid-twentieth century. By 1900, new residents, following the arrival of the railway, had produced an entirely new population mix: only one farmer now remained in the

centre, but several market gardeners and miscellaneous other new occupations had taken their place. The Elm trees formerly on the south side became infected with Dutch elm disease and had to be replaced in 1975. Now the Victorian canopies have gone but other 'street furniture' has appeared, including a pedestrian crossing and roundabout.

ON FORMBY'S 'HIGH STREET' there is now much more traffic. Consideration was given in the 1980s to the idea of 'pedestrianising' the village, a concept abandoned after an experimental trial. People like the 'ambience' and pleasant environment created by the wide pavements and mature trees on both sides of Chapel Lane, as well as the community activities, shops and services of value to the community, the cafés (some open air) and other meeting places. This compact, traditional street scene is still a 'village centre' where you invariably meet friends. There are seats and attractive displays outside some of the small shops, some of which have old-type shop fronts. There is a good selection and balance of mainly individually owned shops, with some specialist traders. It is good that some of the older buildings have been retained and not demolished. Many still retain their traditional signage.

CHAPEL LANE

THE MAIN ROAD through 'the village' was originally called 'Brows Lane' throughout its length. Together with School Lane this can, in many ways, be considered 'the heart' of the village as we know it today. Its dramatic development in the second half of the nineteenth century heralded the expansion of Formby and Freshfield which has continued ever since. The only buildings present in 1845 were seven cottages, four on one side and three on the other, separated by spacious gardens, arable land and meadows. After 1900, new occupations included coal agents, dressmakers, joiners, financial agents, newsagents, chemists, accountants, drapers, confectioners and master butchers.

THE HSBC BANK, formally the Midland Bank, was built in the 1960s alongside traditional nineteenth-century cottages typical of the Victorian period, the last to be occupied – on the north side of Chapel Lane, but still in the old photograph (above) – retaining their original front gardens. Now retail development has occurred on both sides of the bank and all the gardens have gone. At least some trees have survived, however, and these are an attractive feature of the village to this day. The street scene now has a somewhat Continental pavement atmosphere with its bustle of people and through traffic. The last undeveloped space to the west of the bank was finally built on by Marks & Spencer but soon afterwards vacated for bigger premises. At present, the building is unused and for sale.

CHAPEL LANE/
ELBOW LANE CORNER

THE ORIGINAL PHOTOGRAPH was taken at the turn of the twentieth century when the surface of Chapel Lane was being improved by the laying of stone 'setts'. These can still often be unearthed under the modern tarmac. Brows Lane, beyond this corner, was still largely agricultural at that time. Charters' the butcher's, the second shop from the corner, was one of Formby's first butchers: it opened before 1900, and closed in 1998. The cattle and sheep from local farms were originally slaughtered on the premises, to which they were brought 'on the hoof'. William Charters, who was also captain of the fire brigade, celebrated the relief of Ladysmith during the South African War by leading a victory parade through the village on horseback. A less pleasing episode occurred in 1899, when there was a fire at the golf club. Captain Charters, in a one-horse trap, drove around summoning the fireman, but unfortunately the hoses were missing: by the time the firemen arrived, the club had been burnt to the ground!

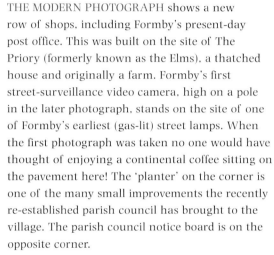

THE MODERN PHOTOGRAPH shows a new row of shops, including Formby's present-day post office. This was built on the site of The Priory (formerly known as the Elms), a thatched house and originally a farm. Formby's first street-surveillance video camera, high on a pole in the later photograph, stands on the site of one of Formby's earliest (gas-lit) street lamps. When the first photograph was taken no one would have thought of enjoying a continental coffee sitting on the pavement here! The 'planter' on the corner is one of the many small improvements the recently re-established parish council has brought to the village. The parish council notice board is on the opposite corner.

CROSS GREEN

THIS WAS ORIGINALLY a triangular area of land at an important intersection of roads, at the heart of the original village but close to the Formby Fields – a very late example of unenclosed strip cultivation (supervised by the Court Leet until the early twentieth century). The date of the original cross is not known. An oak cross 8ft 6in high stood here on a stone base for many years but was replaced by the present sandstone one in 1879. Legend has it that the Downholland Brook could flood to this point. Formby Fair, established in the fourteenth century, was held on the green each year on Oak Apple Day, 29 June. Horses, cattle, sheep and pigs were sold. The diarist Nicholas Blundell of Crosby visited it with his wife in June 1710, together with Mr Anderson of Lydiate, Mr Blundell of Ince and his lady. In 1715 he records a stage play acted there. Nearby, on the corner of Phillips Lane and Liverpool Road, were the village stocks and lock-up.

THIS ANCIENT REMNANT of the village green has, for some reason, never been registered as such and is now generally regarded as just another roundabout. The cottages facing the green have long since gone, and their space is now used as car parking for the adjacent 'Cross House' (formerly Blundell Arms). The wooden railings have also gone, and the Victorian post box has been replaced by a new one in a less vulnerable location. This roundabout is now the busiest in Formby. Roselands, the large house with a 'Mansard' roof, was used during the Second World War as a convalescent home for servicemen and later as a local headquarters for the Red Cross and other voluntary organisations.

THE CROSS HOUSE INN

THIS ESTABLISHMENT WAS formerly known as the Blundell Arms in honour of the Blundells of Ince Blundell, the former joint lords of the manor. Originally a hotel, it overlooks the village green where fairs were held and proclamations made. A small beerhouse originally stood on the site. It was here that the last meetings of the ancient manor court, the Court Leet – which were held up to the early years of the twentieth century and to which 'all persons, particularly sub-tenants, who do suit and service to the court were summoned and required there and then to attend to, do perform the same, and not to depart thence without leave'. A record of one such meeting shows that much of the meeting was taken up by discussion about the state of the numerous watercourses around Formby and their cleansing, which was then the

responsibility of the individual landowners and their tenants. The Cross House had a beautiful bowling green and a commodious range of stables and other outbuildings – all of which have now made way for a car park. Formby also had a chartered market at Cross Green.

THUS FORMBY WAS a well-established trading centre from the fourteenth to the nineteenth centuries. The exterior of the pub has not changed much during the last century, but the inside tells a different story. Those sitting at tables in the bay windows on either side of the front entrance have a marvellous view of the traffic entering Formby at this point! During the summer months the flower beds on the roundabout provide a colourful scene.

THE BAY
HORSE

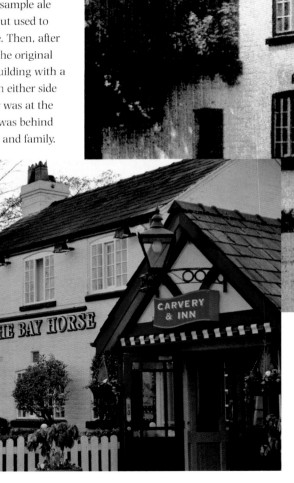

IN 1861 JOHN DICKINSON, aged twenty-six, brewer, farmer (of 12 acres) and beer seller, was living here in a newly erected house called (according to the 1861 census) 'The Bay Pony', together with his wife, Mary, son James, and infant daughter Ann. According to his great grandson, who still lives in Formby, Mr Dickinson – who was in competition with his brothers at Freshfield – was so keen to ensure that his beer was the best in the district that he used to travel in a pony and trap to sample ale at other pubs. He would not go in himself but used to send in his son, still a lad, to get a jug of ale. Then, after a quick glass, he went on to the next one. The original pub was the left-hand part of the present building with a front door in the centre. Two rooms were on either side of a narrow passage and the very small bar was at the rear of the left-hand room. The 'tap-room' was behind this, as were the living quarters for licencee and family.

A PUMP AND trough still stands at the corner of the original house, concealed in the shrubbery. At one time the customers used to haul up the casks from the shallow cellar whose trapdoor was just inside. Changes began in 1956, when landlord Robert Whitehead added the lounge bar and named it 'the Fullerton Lounge' after the triple Waterloo Cup winner. The Withens Lounge was built in the same year. The carvery area which replaced the Withens was built in 1983. The striking weeping ash which stands at the south-east corner of the building is remembered by those who were children here during the Second World War as the 'gum tree', due to its association with visiting American airmen.

THE GRAPES HOTEL

STANDING PROUDLY AT an important corner of Formby's Green Lane conservation area, this handsome building was built in around 1880 and originally included an assembly room. Until the Victoria and Guild Halls were built, any gathering of any size took place here. In 1883 seventy members of the Naturalists Field Club travelled from Exchange Station to Freshfield, and the *Formby Times* reported 'after wandering in a desert [they] met at the Grapes Family

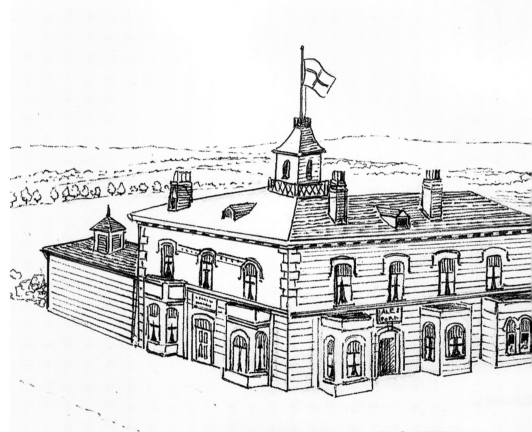

EDWARD JONES
GRAPES FAMILY HOTEL
WINE AND SPIRIT MERCHANT BREWER &
LIVERPOOL AND SOUTHPORT ROAD
FORMBY

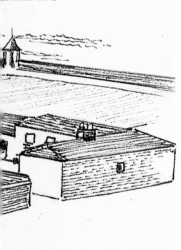

Hotel where tea was served in a handsome room. The proverbial purity of the Formby air on an exceptionally fine day made the excursion highly enjoyable.'

In 1910, pioneer airmen C. Compton Patterson, later to found the South African Air Force, celebrated his first successful flights at Freshfield (accompanied by friend and fellow aviator R.A. King) with a dinner at the Grapes. He made the headlines the next day by flying from Freshfield to Hoylake and back! The licensee, then a Mr Jones, was a wine and spirit merchant and also a brewer. The adjacent building in Ryeground Lane was probably the brewhouse.

THE HOTEL WAS restored in 1978 at a cost of around £200,000 and about eight months' work. Earlier, neighbouring residents had expressed concern: although the building was in a state of disrepair, they wanted its historical features to remain intact. Parking facilities have since been improved – albeit at the expense of bowling enthusiasts, the former green having given way to concrete and tarmac. It took ten years to see the scheme completed but the charm of the old building has been retained. You can still see the beech trees that marked a running track round the bowling green, and the mounting block by the side of the entrance in case you needed any help getting on or off your horse!

RICHARD RIMMER, 'FISH, GAME AND POULTRY DEALER'

RICHARD RIMMER, FISH, game and poultry dealer, also advertised himself as a 'Glass and China Dealer, British and Foreign Fruiterer. Families waited on upon receipt of postcard.' This photograph shows Mr Bill Rimmer as a four year old. He is pictured next to his brother, the late Councillor Jimmy Rimmer OBE, JP, and his father, Mr Richard Rimmer. They pose with various assistants outside the family shop in the village, keeping an eye on their produce. This splendid shop, on the corner of Three Tuns Lane, was apparently photographed just before

Christmas. Approximately 150 Christmas dinners were waiting to be sold, and the Rimmer team look justifiably pleased with their efforts. The Rimmers were a prolific and hard-working family who continued in business until the 1960s. In that decade, one of their other three shops in Chapel Lane was converted in to a small 'supermarket', so starting a major trend in local retailing. Jimmy Rimmer, the head of the family in the period following the 1940s, was very active in local government: he was a local magistrate, and was chairman of the council on three or four occasions.

In the early years of the century, rabbits were an important item of diet and sold for 1s each in the 1950s. Fines for poaching of 'conies' were commonly inflicted by the courts.

IT WOULD BE difficult to imagine a more radical change of use for this corner shop on the main village street. Comparison of these photographs says a lot about changes in lifestyle and retailing. Customers now tend to cross the road to the relatively large supermarket seen behind the trees for their poultry. These would now be sold more oven-ready than the poultry in the earlier photograph. Another change – one which older customers will regret – is the loss of shop assistants with a personal knowledge of their customers' likes and dislikes, with which they were once as familiar as with the things they sold.

THE ELMS

LATER KNOWN AS The Priory, the Elms had a magnificent elm tree in its garden and a large oak front door which led into a most beautiful square hall. The walls were panelled and the staircase made of oak. On the right was a huge fireplace where logs at least 2-3ft long could have been piled up. This interesting nine-bedroom thatched farmhouse appears on the tithe map of 1845, when it was leased by Marjorie Knowles, widow. One of its fields subsequently became

the home of the Formby Football Club, and is now the site of the new swimming pool. The house was renamed by a new owner, Mrs Van den Vord, who had been an air-ferry pilot during the Second World War. She used it as a guest house and tearoom.

In the spring of 1866, a workman renovating a 'hedge bank' (locally known as a 'cop') at the rear of the Elms found a Roman coin in the sandy soil which was subsequently dated to the time of the Emperor Constantine the Great (AD 272-337). Another Roman coin, a silver denarius probably struck before the time of Caesar, was also discovered locally at about the same time.

Many old Formby residents will remember the owner's green parrot, often in a cage in a tree, making piercing 'wolf-whistles' at passers-by.

THE HOUSE WAS re-thatched by a local footballer, then de-thatched and slated. It became damp and degenerated to a poor condition, and was eventually demolished after modern shops had been built alongside it. This row of shops was then extended over the site of the house. It is in this row of shops that the present-day post office is situated. Unfortunately, several of these new shops have now been unused for some time, apparently because of high rental charges.

THE OLD CHURCHYARD

THIS IMAGE WAS drawn in the early 1840s by Catherine Jacson, a granddaughter of the Revd Richard Formby and the author of *Formby Reminiscences*. Her sketch shows the small but ancient graveyard among the sand dunes, on the site of an ancient chapel probably dating from the thirteenth century. The original chapel was abandoned 500 years later, but the graveyard remained. As it was consecrated land, the site continued in use for burials (both Anglican and Roman Catholic). The present-day church, now known as 'the church in the pinewoods', was built in 1852-5 on the edge of the dunes – then without a single pine tree in sight. It still possesses its original Norman font. It stood at a distance from the mid-nineteenth-century

village but close to the then future development of Formby-by-the-Sea. At first the church simply consisted of the present-day nave, but in 1897 a chancel and two vestries were added. A beautiful 'rose window' was also added at the west end in 1898 in memory of Dr Richard Formby, the donor of the site. It depicted local flora, and was designed by the famous artist Edward Reginald Frampton (1872-1923).

A MODERN MEETING room now stands among the trees to the west of the churchyard. Beyond that, enclosed by trees, there is a woodland garden designed to encourage environmental activities, in partnership with St Luke's Primary School and Sefton Coast Ranger service. Being now within the Sefton Coastal Woodland, the church won an 'eco-congregation award' in 2003, 2004 and 2005. Paths have been created, seats put in place, wild flowers transplanted, new daffodils and trees planted and bat boxes and bird boxes put in place. The meeting room now offers refreshment facilities for local walkers and has been named The Lifeboat Café (after the famous remains of Lifeboat House, found nearby).

LEONARD CHESHIRE
HOME, FRESHFIELD

IN 1884 ST PETER'S, Freshfield, a boys' boarding school standing on this site which was
run by a Protestant clergyman, was put on the market. Situated near Freshfield station,
it had views of the open dunes and sea – the Corsican pines had not yet been planted.
In 1877, with the help of the Sisters of the Franciscan Missionaries of St Joseph, Father
Vaughan – then Bishop of Salford, and later to become Archbishop of Westminster – was
instrumental in establishing the building as a junior seminary for boys aged eleven to
seventeen. Many pupils would subsequently move on to train as priests and missionaries.

Originally taking some fifty boys, the house was extended twice: a large, four-storey wing was added in 1928; the institution then housed 120. Due to changing needs it was subsequently closed in 1972.

THE BUILDING WAS then taken over by the Leonard Cheshire Foundation and – with the help of money largely raised by philanthropic local organisations such as the Rotary Club – was converted to meet the needs of its new inhabitants, who were disabled. Although Freshfield proved an ideal site for the Leonard Cheshire foundation, such a large building presented financial and practical problems. For example, it was only possible to use the first floor because of the number of residents in wheelchairs and the cost of maintaining such a large building. After twenty years it was demolished and then replaced by the splendid modern and aesthetically pleasing low-level buildings we see today. These have been designed for thirty-five residents living in private single rooms, or for married couples in two- or three-roomed flats. Wherever practicable, residents are encouraged to lead as independent a lifestyle as they may seek. The employment of an activities organiser has widened horizons, with strong and regular contributions from volunteers and support groups who are considered to be the lifeblood of the foundation.

THE OLD POST MILL

THOUGHT TO DATE from the time of Henry VIII, this fine windmill stood here until 1885 and was owned by the lord of the manor. An interesting condition may be found in the 1772 lease between the miller, Peter Travis, and the Revd Richard Formby: the miller 'will sufficiently keep one pointer or other dog and that he sell to Richard Formby all the meal, seeds, bran, wheat and grain produced by the mill at the market price as demanded in Formby'. In 1793 Peter Travis also had to agree 'to keep the mill in as good condition as it was when he entered into it' – but as the back of the mill was old, Richard Formby agreed to purchase wood providing Peter Travis paid! The revolving wooden structure, known as 'the buck', was supported on a stout wooden post held within a conical brick turret or round-house. The upper structure containing the mechanism and millstones was moved by man or horse to face the wind, by means of a projecting outer tail-pole, supported on a small wheel resting on a circular paved way of stone surrounding the mill. The wooden framing of each sail blade was covered with cloth like a ship's sail, power developing according to the strength of the wind and the area of cloth. Thus the miller trimmed the amount of sail exposed according to wind strength.

A SURVIVING OIL painting suggests that the wooden frames of the sails became rather old and warped before the mill was finally demolished! This happened in the late 1880s and the site was eventually used for the construction of these semi-detached houses. Fortunately the significance of the site has been recognised by the insertion of a plaque commemorating the mill.

DEAN'S COTTAGE

DESPITE BEING A listed building, a demolition order was made in the 1970s for this fifteenth-century cottage to be demolished: it was declared 'unfit for human habitation'. Angry residents mounted a vigorous campaign spearheaded by the Formby Society, who wanted it converted into a folk museum. This is a cruck-framed cottage, erected by splitting tree trunks vertically and standing them together to form inverted 'V's, with a strong beam ridge-pole joining them. The rectangular space between pairs of 'crucks' is known as a 'bay', each usually 16ft in length. This cottage has three bays, with a door opening into the central

room originally open to the rafters. The usual method of enlarging a cruck cottage was to build on additional bays at each end or to add 'lean-tos'.

IT ONCE FRONTED onto Ravenmeols Lane but, having lost its front garden to new housing, it now 'faces' Park Road, adjacent to the Ravenmeols' Community Centre. Until the 1960s it had a very productive nursery garden where local people could readily obtain fresh vegetables. Although it is a Grade II listed building, recent owners have introduced more space. Note the sturdy wooden guttering and the sliding sash windows typical of our traditional local cottages. One of the features that distinguish Formby from other suburban areas is its stock of charming cottages. Most of them are of fragile construction, which leads to their rapid deterioration and eventual collapse if they are not carefully maintained. Dean's Cottage is considered one of the finest examples of cruck construction in this part of the country and is a Grade II listed building. Although the Formby Society successfully prevented its demolition, it lost its campaign to preserve the adjacent area of land between the cottage, Windsor Road and Ravenmeols Lane as a public open space.

WICKS LANE PATH

THE EARLY PHOTOGRAPH (right) was taken during a natural history ramble along Wicks Lane in 1960. This ancient path, which runs from Freshfield Road to the shore, follows an old boundary established between the warrens of the two lords of the manor, Henry Blundell of Ince Blundell and Richard Formby. It was fixed by formal agreement in 1667 and is delineated by a series of cast-iron markers. The westernmost boundary marker is now to be found in the intertidal zone on the foreshore. Wicks Lane is an old route to the sea, probably originally used by fishermen. It apparently takes its name from fields formerly on its north side near its junction with Lark Hill Lane. 'Wicks' was an Anglo-Saxon name for a dairy farm. It seems very likely that rear-dune grassland was formerly used for grazing purposes, as in the nineteenth century there was a cattle pound at the corner with Freshfield Road.

THE LANE WAS cut by the railway in the mid-nineteenth century. There used to be an unmanned level crossing where there is now a footbridge. Formerly, very few houses could be found on the seaward side. An official notice at the level crossing warned drovers of sheep and cattle to open the far gate before allowing their animals to cross the line! Lark Hill Farm is now one of the last asparagus farms in the area, but the farmhouse has recently been demolished to make way for a smart new residence. The new owners of this property on the north side have ensured their privacy not only by erecting a long length of fencing but also by creating an embankment and growing impenetrable hedging. This has completely altered the open character of this old lane. Of the original seven cast-iron boundary markers, now only three are still to be found before the shore is reached.

FORMBY HALL

THIS GRADE II LISTED building is thought to date from the
early sixteenth century. The home of the Formby family for
four centuries, it had a 'facelift' in the early nineteenth century
when its front elevation was changed to the then-fashionable
'Strawberry Hill' neo-Gothic style, with added battlements and
stucco façade. Formby Hall was occupied almost continually
by the manorial family – apart from short periods in the
nineteenth century when it was occupied by tenants – until the
death of the last 'squire', John Frederick Lonsdale Formby, in
1958. As he had lost his two sons during the First World War
he had no direct issue, so the property was settled on a trust.
Shortly afterwards the trustees granted a lease of just over
twenty years to Mr John Moores Jr – who, in turn, allowed the
home to be used by the Brontë foundation, a charity concerned
with providing a recreational home for under-privileged
children from Liverpool.

AFTER THIS, THE house became sadly derelict. In 1988 a
business organisation providing care for the elderly proposed
taking over the building. However, as their plans included a

great deal of additional building, and as the hall, a listed building, was located in the green belt, planning permission was not given. Finally the hall was purchased by a wealthy local businessman and his wife, who, working closely with English Heritage, have successfully restored the building as a private house. Other interesting features include an ancient (listed) dovecote, still relatively intact, but a small building used as a school for village girls for a period has unfortunately been demolished. Most of the demesne land around the hall was purchased for a new private golf club and links, the newest addition to the extensive range of golfing facilities along the Sefton Coast.

OIL WELLS ON FORMBY MOSS

DURING A GEOLOGICAL survey of the moss-land area inland
to Formby in the late 1930s, a number of surface seepages
of petroleum were noted. These had in fact been known
about locally for hundreds of years: one such was originally
described by Camden in 1637 and another by geologists
in 1843. Local people used the dried peat extracted from
the moss land as 'firelighters'. The seepages, rediscovered
in 1937, then led to successful drilling by the D'Arcy
Exploration Co. The first load of 'Formby crude' left by rail
from Preston in June 1939. In 1940, D'Arcy began what was
then to be the deepest well drilled in Britain. Between then
and 1961 the field yielded 9,758 tons (about 75,800 barrels).
Formby was BP's first British oil discovery. Although the flow
was small, it was sufficient to maintain the rigs in economic
service and the Formby field was one of the few operating in
England during the Second World War.

M.E.Sibley.

BY 1966 OPERATIONS were abandoned, the wells were sealed, huts removed and the land restored to its agricultural use. Few signs remain of the once important oilfield, but many older people still remember seeing the 'nodding donkeys' (as the wells were called). Interest still exists in the potential for the area, and now an Aberdeen-based crude petroleum and natural-gas extraction company has again started 'drilling and testing for hydrocarbons on the former oilfield area'. It is thought that, in view of the considerable quantities which have accumulated by seepage in the past, it is very likely that they will get some initial production from shallow depths. The reservoir conditions may, however, have been disturbed by the final actions at the site in 1964, when underground combustion was started to get the remaining oil, which was thicker, to flow to the surface.

'DEATH-DUTY HILL'

THE HIGH DUNES seaward of St Luke's church are known officially as Shorrock's Hill and Beacon Hill. A lantern was hoisted on a mast there when the lifeboat crew were needed, as before the trees were planted it was visible from the village. These dunes were one of the earliest victims of sand-winning. When John Formby, the landowner, found he had death duties to pay in the late 1920s he agreed to the extraction of sand at 6*d* per ton. Sand-winning continued behind the frontal dunes at many different sites and using different hauliers until the mid-1960s. These photographs give some idea of the extent of the sand extraction between Wicks Lane and Lifeboat Road. An even more extensive area is to be found south of Lifeboat Road. Much of this sand was used by iron foundries in the Midlands for casting. A great deal went to Garston for bottle-making and huge amounts to fill sandbags for the protection of Liverpool, and elsewhere, during wartime.

THE RESULTING FLATTENED sandy landscape was, in the nineteenth and early twentieth centuries, found to be ideal for asparagus cultivation and some 200 acres have been used for this by a number of local farmers. This whole rear-dune area was also used extensively by the military during the Second World War. Since then, in conjunction with the several important local nature reserves in the area, it has provided space for visitors to park their cars. A halt to sand-winning came after 1967 when the last approvals were given by the Ministry of Housing and local government – to the dismay of Formby Urban District Council, who had previously refused permission on four grounds: coastal protection and flood prevention; the fact that the sites are of major scientific interest; the fact that the area hosts a nature reserve within the green belt; and, of course, the damage to visual amenity.

FORMBY STATION

THE FIRST PHOTOGRAPH shows Formby Station as it was in the early twentieth century. Because road communication between Liverpool and Southport was so difficult in the mid-nineteenth century, an Act of Parliament was passed in 1847 for the construction of a Liverpool, Crosby and Southport Railway. The first sod was cut on 24 March 1847. The flat nature of the country facilitated quick and cheap construction and the formal opening took place in July of the following year. Formby was one of the original stations, a very modest affair with a level crossing at Duke Street. That station was replaced in around 1880 with the station shown here. It included a house for the stationmaster on the up platform. A road bridge, seen below, was erected to replace the footbridge and adjacent level crossing in the 1930s. A central ticket office was also added.

FORMBY WON THE 'best-kept station garden' in the London Midland Region in 1964, and people travelled to Formby especially to see it. The station regularly won prizes for its tidiness, its gardens and its general attractiveness. Rambling roses grew by the wall under the clock and another by the 'Formby' signs. Sparrows nested year after year in the protective canopy over the platforms and the singing of skylarks in the fields on the seaward side was continuous on sunny days. So too, apparently, was the smell from the piggery if the wind blew from that direction! But despite occasional farmyard smells, Formby had good reason for its pride in its station. Since then there has been considerable loss of facilities, including that of a resident stationmaster, the overhanging canopies to keep waiting passengers dry and coal fires in the waiting rooms during the winter. The most recent intrusion is a huge advertising hoarding overlooking the down platform.

HOLMWOOD SCHOOL

OPENED IN 1901, Holmwood School occupied these purpose-built buildings in 1903, having transferred from smaller premises on the other side of the railway line. It took about 100 boys, most of them boarders, and prepared them for entrance to public schools at age thirteen. It occupied extensive grounds of around 10 acres so had excellent sports facilities. The first headmaster of the school, the Revd C.H.S Gmelin MA, was born in Bengal, India, where his father was a missionary. He returned to England at an early age and was educated at Magdalene College School and Keble College. After graduating he took Holy Orders. An Oxford County Cricketer and Football XI team member, he was an all-round sportsman and

had the distinction of being the first British athlete to compete in Olympic competition in the 1896 Summer Olympics, when he finished third in the inaugural heat of the 100 metres. He did not advance to the final. He was more successful in the 400 metres, however, where he finished second in the preliminary and third in the final. Although no awards were then made for third place, he is usually credited as a bronze-medal winner for finishing just behind US athletes Thomas Burke and Herbert Jamison with a time of 55.6 seconds. Not surprisingly, descriptions of the school put great emphasis on the playing fields, some 6 acres in extent. 'Cricket, rugby and association football carefully taught... There is an excellent rifle range. Boxing, drilling, carpentering, music, dancing and acting [are] particularly encouraged.'

THE SCHOOL PASSED through many phases of expansion. In the 1980s it began to admit girls, but the school closed in the late 1980s. The area has now become another attractive housing estate, with a children's play area close by on a surviving remnant of the former school's playing field.

HARINGTON
BARRACKS, 1946

AFTER THE OUTBREAK of war in 1939, the old depot of the King's (Liverpool) Regiment at Seaforth became inadequate and so was moved 8 miles north to open farmland in Formby, the area where Harington Road is today. New purpose-built barracks were then built, with access from Victoria Road and pedestrian access via Blundell Path, the shortest route to the nearest station. The barracks were named after a former colonel in chief, General Sir Charles Harington GCB CBE DSO MC, who died in 2007. The 13th Kings Regiment moved from here to India in 1942. They then marched into Burma in 1943 with Burmese Gurkha and other British units and became the famed 'Chindits'.

THE KING'S MAIN depot remained here throughout the war, becoming the King's Regiment Infantry Training Centre. Training took place in large gyms, on a large parade ground and on the surrounding open fields. There were football pitches and an athletic ground on the west side of Larkhill Lane (where the National Trust 'Dune Heath' reserve is today). Rifle training started in a covered range situated near where St Jerome's church in Wicks Lane is today. Further practice took place on the (still surviving) open range at the seaward end of Albert Road and finished on Altcar Rifle Range. When relinquished by the army in the early 1960s, the site was acquired by New Ideal Homesteads Ltd. and today's housing estate resulted. Following Local Government reorganisation in 1974, the name 'Harington' was chosen as the name of one of Formby's two new electoral districts. The existence and role in wartime of Harington Barracks, and the existence of very significant military training in and around Formby, is now almost forgotten. It is only commemorated by a small plaque on the wall of the local electricity substation, thought to be the site of the guard room.

CHURCH
ROAD

CHURCH ROAD, LOOKING north. Although in the mid-nineteenth century this was still basically a country lane, Church Road was at this time the main route through Formby. Then, in 1938, construction of the Formby bypass began.

By the beginning of the twentieth century some important buildings were being erected, including the Moorhouse buildings, where the offices of the Formby Urban District Council were at first situated. In 1927 the Moorhouse buildings were replaced by purpose-built council offices in Freshfield Road. Other important buildings nearby included the Queen's Jubilee Hall, later renamed the Guild Hall, and the police station. This was built by the Lancashire Constabulary in 1894, at a cost of £2,074, on land purchased from Revd Lonsdale Formby and John Formby Esq. for the

sum of £100. The building is still in use today. It originally included a small courtroom, a station house for the sergeant and accommodation for a constable. At the rear was a weights and measures office for local tradesmen to have their scales and weights regularly checked.

DURING THE SECOND World War an anti-aircraft gun was also sited at the rear of this building, and rifles were kept ready for use by constables, an armed guard being on duty throughout the war. There were also cells, in one of which a German pilot who had parachuted to safety over Altcar was locked. A mounted section was also based at Formby, using stables at the rear of Chapel Lane and Paradise Lane. Mounted police regularly patrolled the beach and wooded coastal area to check for 'alien' landings. Opposite the police station was White House Farm, which had a dairy herd and some simple cottages (later removed for road widening). Church Road has continued to be developed and redeveloped, the latest addition being a modern fire station.

PINE TREE CAFÉ, FRESHFIELD

THERE ARE JUST two narrow roads leading to the sea at Formby Point: Lifeboat Road (Formby) and Victoria Road (Freshfield). It is strange to realise that, in 1910, at the end of Victoria Road (shown in these two photographs), it was possible for early aviation pioneers to fly their planes from the beach. They used five wooden hangars (sited behind the frontal dunes and farm horses) to drag the planes out! The beach was for several years officially recognised as an aerodrome. The Pine Tree Café which later stood here was probably originally erected during the Second World War, as it is known that there was military activity (including a concrete pillbox) at this important

site overlooking Liverpool Bay. For many years after the war the building was used as a tearoom, a welcome provision for many walkers.

IN 1964 THE seaward end of Victoria Road, together with 400 acres of dunes and woodland, was taken over by the National Trust, under 'Enterprise Neptune'. Unfortunately, the acreage managed by the Trust has been slowly diminishing since then due to erosion. Much of this area has now been reclaimed by the sea, aided by strong westerly onshore winds. 'Blow outs' form, which then move inland on the windward side of the dune crest. 'Visitor-pressure' exacerbates this effect by trampling on the Marram Grass. The presence of this type of grass, as has been known for centuries, helps to stabilise the dunes. For this reason Marram is replanted from time to time. Wooden fences also help prevent erosion and, in addition, during the last few years discarded Christmas trees have made useful windbreaks. Last winter, several thousand dead trees were 'planted'.

THATCHED HOUSES, DUKE STREET

THIS PHOTOGRAPH SHOWS the view of Duke Street as you head towards the station from Elbow Lane. These previously thatched houses are on the north side of the road, overlooking the area which is now Duke Street Park. In the 1851 census the occupation of the inhabitants was given as fishermen or farmers. The occupants would have had large back gardens, used for growing vegetables.

Until the mid-twentieth century Formby had very many thatched cottages and even a few thatched houses. It is said that thatch remained the only roofing material available to the bulk of the population in the countryside in many towns and villages until the late 1800s. In this

area Welsh slate became available after 1820 and roofing tiles much later. The number of thatched properties actually increased during the mid-1800s as agriculture expanded. The decline began at the end of the nineteenth century. Good quality straw thatch can last more than half a century: new layers of straw were simply applied over the weathered surface of the old. Good quality straw has unfortunately declined since the introduction of the combine harvester and the release of short-stemmed wheat varieties. The increased use of nitrogen fertiliser in the 1960s and 1970s has also weakened straw and reduced its longevity.

THESE HOUSES HAVE survived to the present day – and indeed include an additional extension on the east end, at one time a shop. Their thatch has now been replaced with a tiled roof; new windows have been inserted and the 'wonky' chimney replaced. The fields behind have now been extensively developed. Unfortunately, thatched houses are harder to insure and it is more expensive to re-thatch a roof than to replace it with slate or tiles. It is, however, good to realise that old cottages can be successfully renovated and continue to make characterful homes.

FORMBY-BY-THE-SEA

UNTIL THE LATE nineteenth century there was little development of Formby, or its neighbouring manor of Ravenmeols, to the west of the Liverpool-Southport Railway line. However, in 1875 the Formby Land and Building Co. attempted to create a new residential area and seaside resort here 'to rival Southport'. Despite construction of a promenade between 1876 and 1888, only a few houses were built and the dual-level promenade was soon overwhelmed by blown sand. It still exists, completely buried under the dunes. A loop line was planned to connect this development with the Liverpool-Southport Railway but not constructed.

FORTUNATELY FOR THE natural coast, the impetus for the scheme was lost and only a handful of houses were built. The small boy in the photograph lived in one called 'Seabank House', overlooking the promenade. The main part of this property was for many years used to provide

seaside holidays for poor Liverpool children and was known
as Father Berry's Home. That small boy, Philip Clulee, is now
in his nineties and is in fact the oldest member of the Formby
Civic Society. Formerly an important local businessman and
well-known Rotarian, he founded a local organisation to
help disabled people appreciate art. During the Depression
of the 1930s, a number of the other roomy houses, built
to attract visitors, were – like Seabank House – acquired by
various philanthropic organisations to provide holidays for
poor children from Liverpool, Bootle, Manchester and Salford.

During the Second World
War these properties were
all requisitioned by the army,
and most were left in rather
poor condition. In the 1970s
the area was purchased from
the Formby family trustees by
developers with the intention
of converting it into a golf
course. This was opposed by
local people and it was finally
acquired by Sefton MBC and
became officially recognised as
a nature reserve.

BISHOP'S COURT
SCHOOL

BISHOP'S COURT SCHOOL was a preparatory school for boys
in Wrigley's Lane. It was founded in 1892 by Miss Emma
Gosford, the principal, at the request of Bishop Whiteside,
then Roman Catholic Bishop of Liverpool, the first official
visitor. Consequently the school, then with about forty pupils,
was named after him. Until 1924 the school was based in the
now-demolished Vaughan House in Victoria Road, but it moved
in 1924 to Wrigley's Lane, the former home of a family of that
name. It was later extended by the addition of an attractive
'Arts and Crafts' wing. Prize-giving ceremonies were held in the
Victoria Hall, with music, songs and a display; these were under
the direction of Mr Bullen, the drill master, who remained on the
staff for forty-eight years. The school had a very strong Scout
group started during the First World War. A scrapbook has been
preserved with many early photographs of the boy's activities,
including handwritten notes on the history of the school, and
military distinctions of former pupils. A set of postcards has also
survived showing the interior of the school and classes in action.

IN 1967 THE school was taken over by the Augustinian Fathers of the Vice-Province of England and Scotland. Among Bishops Court's old boys was Father Martin D'Arcy, the writer, scholar and former head of the English Jesuits. In 1977 the school became co-ed following the closure of several Catholic girls' schools in the area. By then a number of prefabricated classrooms had been erected around the school, together with an outdoor swimming pool, a sports hall, a squash court, three rugby pitches and a cricket pitch.

Unfortunately there is now no trace left of this building, which was replaced in the early 1980s by the pleasant suburban residential development shown here.

OUR LADY'S SCHOOL

THE THEN JOINT lord of the manor Thomas Weld-Blundell originally gave the land (previously the site of two cottages and their gardens) for this school, built at a cost of £1,200 in 1871. Until that time there was no Roman Catholic school in Formby, despite the large number of Roman Catholic families traditionally living here. The impetus for the building of this school was undoubtedly due to the strong educational interests of the Revd James Carr, parish priest of Formby for over fifty years. He first came to Formby in 1861 and in 1863 witnessed the laying of the foundation stone of a Roman Catholic church. In 1880

he became Diocesan Inspector of Schools and Training Colleges for teachers in England and Scotland. The school was extended in 1888, and in 1895 an infants' room was added. There was a further extension about 1900 when it was taken over by Lancashire Education Authority. Gas lighting remained, however, until 1963, when the rising school population necessitated the building of a new school at Bull Cop.

AFTER DEMOLITION OF the old school buildings, the erection of sheltered flats and houses on the site was approved in 1986. This marked a change of policy, as previously only two-storey developments in Formby had been approved. This scheme cost around £750,000 and provided thirty-two elderly persons' flats, one warden's flat and one guest flat, accepted as a much-needed development. This planning permission was then followed in the subsequent quarter century by the approval and construction of many other large and privately constructed apartment blocks. Liverpool Road was relatively quiet when these photographs were taken, but it was once the main road between Liverpool and Southport. It was finally superseded by the creation of the Formby bypass in the 1930s.

FORMBY COUNCIL OFFICES

ON 8 FEBRUARY 1952 crowds gathered at Formby Council Offices in Freshfield Road to hear the then chairman of the Formby Urban District Council, Peggy Beeston, make the official proclamation of Queen Elizabeth II's accession to the throne.

This imposing building had been formally opened in 1927, replacing the previous council offices in Moorhouse Buildings, Church Road. The project cost £6,200 and the building was designed by Major F.A. Roome, a Formby resident. The original design was 'such that a further wing can be added with the minimum of cost'. It was 'a building reflecting the old historical atmosphere combined with the simple quiet dignity required of a public building.' Internal decoration was supervised by the then chairman of the council, Mr Holden. For seventy-three years it was the hub of municipal life in Formby, until local government reorganisation led to the creation of Merseyside County Council and Sefton Borough Council in 1974. During that time the council offices were

fully used: they housed council meetings and magistrates' courts; were the main base for Sefton Coastal Management Team and Coastal Ranger Service; and provided an outpost for planning, education and finance. On several occasions the building's possible use as a civic centre was seriously discussed. It retained many interesting mementoes – maps, plaques, etc. – relating to Formby's history, particularly during the Second World War, and even in its later, neglected state reflected Formby's long existence as a special place on what was then part of the Lancashire Coast.

UNFORTUNATELY, IN AUGUST 2000 Sefton Council decided to demolish this fine old building and sell the site. It was strongly felt at the time that this decision had been made without adequate public consultation but an appeal was rejected and the 4-acre site was purchased by developers who proceeded to construct a three-storey residential apartment block, called Hillary Court.

THE WICKS LANE LAKE

THIS IS AN unexpected area of open water in what is otherwise a fairly arid landscape at Formby Point. The lake lies in the north-west corner of the Lifeboat Road site, on the south side of the Wicks Lane footpath. There is no lining or base to the lake and the level of water is simply the natural groundwater level. This explains why the lake can be almost dry in the autumn and flooded in the spring. The lake was artificially excavated in 1978 as part of the Formby Point landscape restoration project. Creating the lake solved a local problem of sand blow and also provided an inland paddling pool. The paddling pool was immensely popular and attracted many

local children but unfortunately the water quality did not meet the stringent requirements for freshwater and so, rather than infilling the lake, it was converted into a wildlife haven.

THE LAKE WAS re-profiled in 1987, the bridge constructed and some trees and pond vegetation added. Eight years later the lake is a flourishing wildlife site and a special place on the Sefton Coast. It has minimal management: just some coppicing of the trees and shrubs surrounding it, as well as litter-picking and bin-emptying. Sefton Coast and Countryside would like to do some work on keeping the lake open by removing some of the emergent vegetation on the western side in particular and have recently repaired the bridge. The water level fluctuates somewhat with the water table. It is not a suitable breeding site for the Natterjack Toad, but does get some dragonflies and other more common pond creatures. It has become very popular with families feeding the ducks – which is not conducive to good water quality but is very much enjoyed by visitors (and ducks!).

ANDREWS LANE

WHEN THESE HOUSES were built there was little residential property on the west side of the railway line. Andrews Lane seems to have originally been a sandy track. Local legend has it that it was named after a person of that name who had a fine orchard. In the mid-nineteenth century there was just a single cottage on it, at the 'Clayholes', but the land fronting this portion of Andrews Lane was purchased from the Formby family by the Formby Land and Property Co. for development in the late nineteenth century, as part of its 'Formby-by-the-Sea' project.

The company's stated intention was:

...the laying out, forming, and sewering of streets, roads, parks, gardens, squares, crescents, terraces, boulevards, Promenades and other open spaces; the making of piers, jetties, and landing places in, upon and connected with lands purchased; the laying of tramways, railways, and running carriages thereon ... the forming of waterworks and reservoirs, for supplying water; the erection of gasworks, and the manufacture of gas and the selling of the same; the erection of markets, docks, hotels, laundries, baths, water gardens, aquariums; the manufacture of bricks and tiles.

UNLIKE THE TWO other sections, including the sea-side resort, this eastern section, of 48 acres, bounded by Queens Road, Jubilee Road, Barton Heys Road and Andrews Lane, was successfully developed in the late nineteenth century, apparently by a number of different builders. It succeeded because of its proximity to Formby Station.

Apart from the construction of the Promenade and a scattering of resort-type houses on two roads closer to the sea, the company signally failed in the remainder of its ambitious objectives.

INCE BLUNDELL HALL

THE BLUNDELL FAMILY acquired three quarters of the manor of Formby in the eighteenth century, the remaining quarter being retained from a very early period by the Formbys of Formby Hall. Ince Blundell Hall, described by Pollard and Pevsner as 'a splendid Georgian house with attendant temples', was started by Robert Blundell in around 1720 but was improved and enlarged by his son Henry in the 1760s – 'without the help of any architect', he claimed! Henry also enclosed the park with a tall encircling park wall, pierced by two splendid gateways, and built the recently restored Garden Temple and the Pantheon seen on the right of the

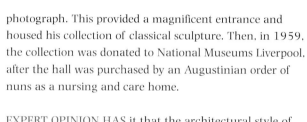

photograph. This provided a magnificent entrance and housed his collection of classical sculpture. Then, in 1959, the collection was donated to National Museums Liverpool, after the hall was purchased by an Augustinian order of nuns as a nursing and care home.

EXPERT OPINION HAS it that the architectural style of the house was inspired by Buckingham House, London, core of today's palace but originally a large townhouse built for the Duke of Buckingham in 1705. The hall is surrounded by extensive parkland complete with lawns, ha-ha, and mature belts and clumps of trees. It is available to the local schools for retreat days, nature walks etc. Local schools provide concerts on occasions for the residents, and the nursing home is used for school placements where pupils gain work experience. Colleges of Further Education conduct horticultural workshops and training in the extensive grounds. The grounds are also open to art schools and 'quiet days' are arranged by local parish groups of all denominations. Exhibitions are held in the Pantheon, where paintings, crafts and other works of art are displayed in this unique setting (which is also the venue for many concerts).

COASTAL EROSION

DURING THE LAST century, the long sandy belt of dunes around Formby Point, with its unique flora and fauna, has been threatened by erosion. There are two natural causes for this: wind and wave action. The other (theoretically more manageable) cause is human trampling. The Sefton Coast has now one of the highest levels of visitor pressure of any major European sand-dune system. It has been known for centuries that the stability of the dune surface can be improved by the planting of Marram Grass and local tenants were obliged in the past by their tenancy agreements to regularly assist with this to improve dune stability. This is now done regularly by volunteers and staff and has been fairly successful. Neither this nor

the plantation of pines can reduce the effects of wave action, however, which is unrelentingly causing loss of frontal dunes at Formby Point, the eroded sand being shifted by the tidal currents both north and south.

IT IS NOW seen that the natural mobility of the coast can not be halted but may be slowed by the reduction of visitor pressure. This can be assisted by improved public understanding of the coastal environment. A visitor centre at Formby Point is badly needed to assist with education and advice as well as provision of much-needed amenities. Loss and destruction of the natural dune habitat also occurred during the previous century by sand-winning and tipping of nicotine waste. Protection of the dune frontage has been aided by the use of brushwood and split-chestnut post and wire fencing and the provision of boardwalks.

A PLOUGHING TEAM
AT KIRKLAKE BANK

THE 'KIRK LAKE' was a shallow lake inland to the dunes and close to the site of a medieval chapel, an early chapel of the parish of Walton-on-the-Hill. This location is very close to the coast and is therefore sandy. However, since the nineteenth century it has been sheltered by a pine plantation from the prevailing westerly winds.

This particular area was formerly used mainly for grazing, only a small area being arable. Up to the nineteenth century a medieval pattern of land use was still in existence. Rye was grown. This had a long stalk which was excellent for thatching. This photograph was taken fairly close to St Luke's church, on a site very close to the original chapel and a group of residences of several descendants of the manorial families. Because of the poor agricultural quality of much of their land, they recognised that after the coming of the railway the area would be suitable for residential development, and of course more profitable than farming for them!

CONSEQUENTLY, THESE FIELDS are now covered by pleasant modern housing whose owners enjoy the advantage of easy access to the open coast on the one hand and the railway on the other. Kirklake Bank was the site of an interesting house of that name built in around 1864 and occupied for many years by members of the Formby family. Finally demolished in 1972, its site (shown here) is still surrounded by trees, both pine and deciduous. The undulating nature of the terrain indicates its proximity to the coast and the underlying dunes. Not surprisingly, the trees lean away from the sea.

ALTCAR RIFLE RANGE

ORIGINALLY CALLED HIGHTOWN Rifle Range, this range is situated at the mouth of the River Alt. Land, on both sides of the river near its original mouth, has been reclaimed, and the range includes 20 acres reclaimed from the sea in the late eighteenth and early nineteenth centuries. It was first used as a private 'Rifle Training Ground' by the 5th Lancashire Rifle Volunteer Brigade, formed by Lieutenant-Colonel Robert Gladstone at his own expense (but with the support of Lord Sefton, the main land owner in 1860).

Originally the range had just one target as a 'firing point', situated at 1,100 yards distance. The first round, from an Enfield muzzleloader (.577 inch), was fired by Lord Sefton. Further targets and firing points quickly followed and later the land was transferred to the West Lancashire Territorial Association. Soon there were thirty targets available – ten more than those at Wimbledon range, which was used by the National Rifle Association. By 1883 the number of targets had again increased to ninety-six, and two years later it was agreed that the range could be used by the regular army.

ALTCAR TRAINING CAMP is now managed by the Reserve Forces and Cadets Association for the North West of England and the Isle of Man. It is one of the UK's premier facilities for small-arms marksmanship training.

As part of the Sefton Coast, the area is also a sanctuary for wildlife from the foreshore danger-area, giving protection to thousands of passage and overwintering birds. The dunes are also home to internationally protected species such as the sand lizard and the Natterjack Toad. The grasslands, originally coastal marshland, support spectacular displays of wild flowers, and in May and June the ranges are covered in a pink haze of orchids and Ragged Robin, with scattered yellow patches of cowslips. (Courtesy of Lt.-Col Michael Cook, MBE, TD)

HOLY TRINITY CHURCH

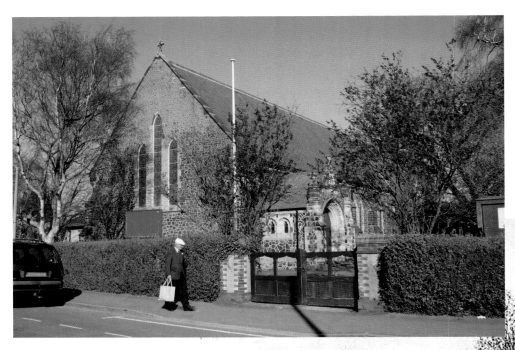

BETWEEN 1855 AND 1885, the population of Formby quadrupled. By 1885 it was felt that the population of Formby had grown to such an extent that a further Anglican church was needed. It was also felt that the two existing Anglican places of worship were 'out of the way'. A portion of land closer to the centre of the village, in Rosemary Lane, was therefore donated by a member of the Formby family, the Revd Lonsdale Formby. In 1888 plans for the nave were approved. The foundation stone was laid the following year.

Holy Trinity church nave was built using white 'Stourton' stone from Storeton in the Wirral and

blue-grey granite from Penmaenmawr. The Revd J.B. Richardson from County Monaghan, a graduate of Trinity College, Dublin, and a keen cricketer, football and athlete, was chosen as the first vicar. The church was opened on Trinity Sunday, 1 June 1890. In 1893 a new parish was formed from the existing parish of Walton-on-the Hill.

THE FOLLOWING YEAR, efforts were made to raise funds to complete the church with the addition of chancel, transepts, belfry and organ, a fund-raising fair being held at Shaftesbury House. This set the scene for further successful fundraising concerts. In 1898 they were assisted by the vicar's cousin, Percy French, with 'music, witty tales, and songs accompanying himself on the banjo'. Percy French gave further fundraising entertainments in 1905, 1908 and 1910. In 1909 the parish hall was opened, replacing a previous wooden hut. The hall was used as a recreation centre for troops from Altcar and Hightown during the First World War and has remained an important facility and meeting place for many groups and societies ever since. A lay pastoral care team was set up in 1986. Holy Trinity has always been outward looking, as evidenced by its adjacent tennis and bowls clubs, and Formby Theatre Club.

SHAFTESBURY HOUSE

THIS WAS A private residence in Ravenmeols Lane until 1888, when it was rented by a
Dr Stanley Gill as a private mental hospital. Dr Gill, its resident physician, added additional
accommodation on both wings of the original house and claimed that its plan was 'approved
by the Commissioners in lunacy in every possible way'. Situated about a mile from the sea,
patients had the benefit of sea air, private rooms, special attendants and accommodation
for visitors. Surrounding the house, there were 10 acres of ornamentally laid-out pleasure
grounds 'providing ample privacy and room for exercise, lawn tennis and other amusements'.
Dr Gill had previously been the superintendent of the Royal Liverpool Lunatic Asylum: this

closed in 1881 when he opened a private asylum in Wavertree. After the Wavertree institution closed, in 1888, he transferred his patients to Shaftesbury House. Commissioners' reports were said to be 'generally favourable': the only failing was the inadequacy of the library, which consisted of just five books, all of a religious nature!

SHAFTESBURY HOUSE HAD as its chaplain the Revd J.B. Richardson, vicar of Holy Trinity (whose cousin Percy French, as previously mentioned, entertained local people in its large hall to successfully raise funds for Holy Trinity church).

The property was taken over by Merseyside Catholic Social Services in 1949 to provide a home for thirty boys moved from an earlier home in Everton Crescent, Liverpool, established in 1859. These boys were disturbed, maladjusted, beyond parental control, educationally subnormal or delinquent – but it was hoped that Shaftesbury House would provide a 'homely atmosphere combined with promotion of full physical and intellectual ability and stability of temperament'. Unfortunately, however, the building became very dilapidated and, in 1988, faced with the prospect of a huge repair bill, the directors decided to evacuate the building. It was subsequently demolished and replaced by yet another pleasant housing estate.

WILSON'S GARAGE

THIS, THE FIRST garage in Formby, was established by Tom Wilson in 1910, standing on the left in the above photograph. Born in 1884 at Grange-over-Sands, he served an engineering apprenticeship with Vickers-Armstrong in Barrow-in-Furness and subsequently sailed as a ship's engineer to South America. After arriving in Formby he did light engineering, agricultural and cycle repairs and even repaired some of the pioneer aircraft then flying from the shore at Freshfield: the beach being officially recognised as an aerodrome in 1910 to 1912.

TOM, WHO WAS steeped in motoring history, handed over to his son-in-law Phil Clulee in 1950. Phil later established the Formby Coach Co. as a parallel business. Phil, born in 1916, first came to Formby at the age of two, living with his parents at Seabank House, Formby-by-the-Sea.

In the 1930s Phil worked with the D'Arcy Exploration Co. on the Formby oilfield, the only one operational in Britain during the Second World War. During the war, when he was a motorcycle dispatch rider, he served in France and Belgium, before being evacuated back to Britain via Dunkirk. He remained in the Army until 1945. As a dispatch rider he sometimes found himself behind the German front line. As a motor coach-owner/driver, his most outstanding feat was in 1967, when he drove a party of students 5,000 miles from Formby into Poland and Russia and back. Phil retired in 1982 when the business was sold to John Chapman and George Mawdsley. George continues to run it now.

MOSS SIDE

UNTIL RECENTLY, THIS quiet rural
corner had changed little over the years.
Going towards Ormskirk, you passed
old cottages on the south side and then
over a bridge guarded by white rails.
Further on, at the Formby-Downholland
boundary, there is another bridge taking
the lane over Downholland Brook
and onto the moss. Sometime in the
last century, Downholland Brook was
straightened at this point. For a very long
time it has been the boundary between
Formby and Downholland civil parishes.
At one time one of the cottages near to
the brook was an ale house called the
Ship Inn – very welcome for farm workers
and travellers! During the last decade
many of the original old cottages and
farms have either been demolished or

renovated almost out of all recognition. It remains, however, a relatively quiet and pretty corner of Formby. The old course of Downholland Brook is carefully tended and its grassy banks now look manicured. Some of the old willows have gone and you no longer have to slow down whilst groups of domestic ducks and geese cross the lane...

THE WOODEN RAILS have been replaced by metal ones and the bridge widened to facilitate the increased traffic across the moss. Peat, formerly a very valuable fuel for Formby cottagers, is no longer extracted from the moss, which is now drained and intensively cultivated. Formerly it would have been covered with sheets of water during the winter months, drying out during the summer when selected areas became used, and valued for summer grazing. Unfortunately, however, because of the relative lack of easily recognised landmarks in the moss-land landscape, there were frequent disputes between the lords of the manor and their tenants regarding rights to turbary (peat cutting) and pasturage. One of these disputes, in 1557-9, necessitated the drawing up of a detailed map, a copy of which now hangs in Formby Library.

FRESHFIELD BOWLING CLUB

FOUNDED IN 1894 and usually referred to as 'the Tin Tab', this private bowling club is seen here acting as 'host' to convalescent soldiers during the First World War. The original members, seeking a suitable clubhouse, eventually located a disused, former Congregational church which was already known by that nickname – short, of course, for tabernacle. When the building was moved to its present site, the name stuck. The clubhouse is now steeped in memories of past officials and past achievements. Photographs of previous presidents are featured on the walls. Visitors can also see a bar stock list from February 1899, when beer was sold at 1s 9d per dozen bottles; a gallon of whisky was all of 17s, while a box of cigars cost 14s 6d for 100. The club is

strictly 'men only'. Ladies are invited into the clubhouse on only two occasions each year: the chairman's social and the president's night. Some of the older members feel that even this is too much! Only one woman's name appears in the visitors' book: this was added on 14 June 1947, when the famous actress Margaret Rutherford, daughter-in-law of a past president, visited. It is not recorded whether she played!

THE CLUB HAS always been a 'haven of rest' for local businessmen and still maintains this atmosphere: a place to relax, meet friends and converse. The old photographs on the walls often prompt discussion about the past, which can be very enlightening for the newer members. Apart from bowls, the club offers a number of facilities: snooker; darts; dominoes; draughts, chess, cards and shove halfpenny are also played. Bowling does not normally take place on a competitive basis, but more as a pleasant pastime, although the club does hold two tournaments per year.

FORMBY LIGHTHOUSE

FORMBY LIGHTHOUSE WAS one of the earliest nautical structures erected to help aid navigation and safety at the Port of Liverpool. It was erected soon after the opening of the first dock. Nicholas Blundell noted in his diary on the 17 September 1719 that his wife and he 'rode out to see the landmark as it is building'. Although now remembered as a lighthouse, the structure – which survived until it was destroyed by the military in 1941 – was actually only used as a lighthouse for a relatively short part of its life. The rest of the time it stood overlooking the dangerous approaches to the river as a simple landmark. It worked in conjunction with a lower mark, the position of which had to be altered from time to time due to the changing courses of the natural channels. It was the port's first marine surveyor, Denham, who arranged for the tower's conversion into a lighthouse in 1831, following a very thorough survey of the Mersey approaches. Working with a new Formby light vessel, the building guided shipping through the new channel.

THE COST OF conversion came to £300, which included an attached dwelling for the keeper and £40 for a light reflector. The keeper, appointed at a salary of £20 per annum, was also put in charge of the already well-established Formby Lifeboat Station. It ceased to be a lighthouse for a period following 1839, but the tower was lit again between 1851 and 1856. After this date, the light was removed to a new lighthouse at Crosby. The site is within the grounds of Altcar Rifle Range, but we visited in July 2010. Nothing remains of the structure, but the site has now been marked by a specially designed marker post, kindly provided by Altcar Training Camp.

THE LIFEBOAT STATION

FORMBY HAD THE very first lifeboat station in the world. It was established by the Liverpool Dock Committee, under the leadership of dock master William Hutchinson, before 1776. The Liverpool Bay Lifeboat Service later included five other stations scattered around the Mersey approaches. They continued as an independent service until the service was finally taken over by the RNLI in the late nineteenth century.

During the period that the Formby Lighthouse was 'lit', its superintendent was also put in charge of the lifeboat. Lt. Walker tragically lost his life when the lifeboat capsized during the rescue attempt of a disabled pilot vessel in a severe gale in 1836. For his heroic assistance on this occasion the village doctor, Richard Sumner, won the gold medals of the Royal Humane Society and of the 'Shipwreck Institution', the forerunner of the RNLI, for successfully swimming out to the wrecked vessel and rescuing some of the crew.

AFTER THE STATION was finally closed in 1918, the site was encroached by the dunes. For many years it was used as a tearoom. John Aindow Jr, one of the crew, remained in the lifeboat cottage behind the station. He was employed by Liverpool Dock Committee to read the tide-poles every fifteen minutes during daylight hours until he, in turn, handed over his duties to Joseph Aindow. Mr Aindow left the cottage upon its demolition. It was finally dismantled at the same time as the boathouse, in 1965, but now – as can be seen – tidal erosion has brought the high-water line right back to the surviving remains of the building. The building itself was finally demolished in the 1970s as it was deemed to be in a dangerous condition. Unfortunately this happened before research revealed the great historical significance of this site.

ALTMOUTH PUMPING STATION

THIS SERVES A total catchment area of 89 square miles, including 20 square miles of rich agricultural moss land. Tidal gates built in 1779 gradually fell into disrepair until, in 1830, there was a 'blow out' under the foundations. A new structure was then built downstream. This structure was improved in 1933 by the addition of three smaller gates, but was replaced in 1972 by this new station, one of the country's biggest, with a pumping capacity of over 1 million gallons per minute.

All the station's pumping equipment is electrically powered; there are four dry weather flow pumps and four storm pumps with combined nominal capacities of $6.56\text{m}^3/\text{s}$ and $54\text{m}^3/\text{s}$, respectively. When all its pumps are in action, the station is capable of discharging approximately 60 tons of water per second into Liverpool Bay. Also instilled is a backup 2.5MW diesel electric generator capable of running the four storm pumps and possibly one dry weather flow pump. The weed screen has two grabs, delivering debris to opposite banks.

THE STATION WAS designed to give protection for the moss land by keeping river levels below danger level in the embanked sections during the worst conditions of combined storm and high tide that are likely to occur once in about fifty years. After forty years of use, this pumping station – originally one of the most powerful in Europe – is now nearing the end of its life. Considerable discussion has been taking place over the last few years regarding the design and specification for a replacement system.

The whole approach to grassland drainage has recently been revised and in the future there will be a greater tendency to allow flood water to be 'stored' in low-lying 'overspill' storage areas. This approach has the approval of natural historians as it might provide a return to original wildlife conditions.

VICTORIA ROAD FROM FRESHFIELD STATION

WHEN HARINGTON BARRACKS was relinquished by the army in the early 1960s the site was acquired by 'New Ideal Homesteads Ltd'. Their brochure included this view from Freshfield Station footbridge, showing Victoria Road running towards the sea. They promised that 'in almost every case a garage or space for one car' was intended. This estate was the first of many subsequent local developments.

THIS, THE NOW most heavily used route to the shore and pine-woods by both pedestrians and cars, did not exist at all until the late nineteenth century, when some large houses started to be built around Freshfield Station. This station was originally constructed at the request of Thomas Fresh, Liverpool's 'inspector of nuisances', who had previously had a 'manure-siding' created at the site to facilitate the transfer of 'night-soil' to local farmers wanting to improve

the fertility of the sandy soils of the area. The then dominant landowner saw potential to develop the area as a wealthy resort, even to the extent of providing a pier. That did not happen, but the coastal dune area was extensively managed for asparagus cultivation and the track to Jimmy Lowe's former Pine Tree (Asparagus) Farm has, since 1964, been owned by the National Trust and becomes busy with traffic during fine weekends and the summer months. One of the main attractions – and also of great ecological value – is the fact that these relatively isolated pine woods provide ideal conditions for the local red squirrel population. Unfortunately, many of the original and rather grand Victorian houses in Victoria Road have been replaced by closer-spaced but still expensive smaller properties, some now owned by famous footballers.

FROM THE STATION GATE TO-

THE OLD SCHOOL

THIS SCHOOL, WHICH gave its name to the lane, was originally established in 1659 when the inhabitants of Formby obtained permission from the lord of the manor to erect a school on some waste land. The villagers collected money for the building of the school and the lord of the manor, Mr Blundell, gave the land for a peppercorn rent of 1s per annum. Trustees were appointed to manage the school, appointing masters and keeping the fabric and repair at the expense of the township. There were, however, difficulties in paying the schoolmaster and by 1688 the building had been standing vacant for several years. It recommenced in 1703 with funding from a new

charity (Marsh's Charity), set up for the purpose by a Mr Richard Marsh, a London merchant who had been brought up in Formby. Mr Marsh left an endowment of £400, which seems to have revived the school for a period. In 1711 there were two masters, a headmaster and an assistant.

THE VILLAGE SCHOOL was at first intended for girls as well as boys but the income was not sufficient to keep it going. The Formby family then provided schools for a period at locations adjacent to the hall. The original building was demolished in 1785 and replaced by the present building, which dates from that time. It is thus over 200 years old. By the mid-nineteenth century the need for better schools became apparent, and St Peter's Junior School in Paradise Lane came into being, again funded by the Formby family. In a poor state of repair, the old school was for many years used as a cottage, and designated as a Grade II listed building. However, in the early 1980s the building was converted into a restaurant by a Mr Kicki Kakou. It has remained a restaurant and listed building ever since.

FRESHFIELD DUNE HEATH

THE DUNES AND sandy heaths of the Sefton Coast have produced excellent golf courses. Many are still flourishing after many years. However, the Freshfield Golf Club (or more correctly, the Banking and Insurance Golf Cub), pictured here, had a relatively brief life. During 1941 this course, together with its clubhouse and neighbouring farmland, was requisitioned for RAF Woodvale. The clubhouse became the Polish Officers' Mess but was demolished after the war. RAF Woodvale is one of the last Second World War emergency fighter aerodromes still in use. Nowadays it is primarily the base of the Manchester, Salford and Liverpool Universities' RAF Air Squadrons, but a gliding squadron and the Merseyside Police Air Support Helicopter also use it.

ONE PERIPHERAL AREA has not been actively used since the Second World War and, having remained protected within the airfield perimeter fence, has reverted to dune heathland, nowadays a rare but valuable natural habitat. Freshfield Dune Heath now has 35ha of lowland, acidic grassland, woodland and scrub, the largest area of lowland heath in Lancashire. This site comprises 9 per cent of the national total of this very rare habitat. As such, it was taken over by the Lancashire, Manchester and North Merseyside Wildlife Trust in 2006. Animals now graze on it to maintain its ecological status. Another 4ha of dune heath is located just outside the perimeter fence. This contains the site of the former clubhouse, and was the subject of a planning application for a housing development in 1972. Fortunately, however, this was refused. The reserve is now open to the public: a path has been created around it but flying still continues on the airfield south of the reserve. Sadly, however, the extensive heather formerly covering the rest of the airfield periphery has been cleared.

OPEN AIR ART EXHIBITION

ORGANISED BY THE Formby Civic Society, the Open Air Art Exhibition has been held under the old village chestnut trees as a regular and colourful feature of village life each June since the early 1950s. Local artists have recorded with pen, brush and camera the many old cottages, farms, lanes and landscapes representative of Formby's past, producing valuable records of many interesting buildings; some of these have stood for hundreds of years, but many, alas, have now vanished. One local artist in particular, Muriel Sibley, recorded many of the local thatched cottages. Her records are not limited to line drawings or watercolours, as for each of her subjects she also took a number of high-quality transparencies – about 2,000 subjects in total. Anxious that her works should be preserved as a historical record, Muriel bequeathed her collection to the Formby Civic Society, along with her personal notes.

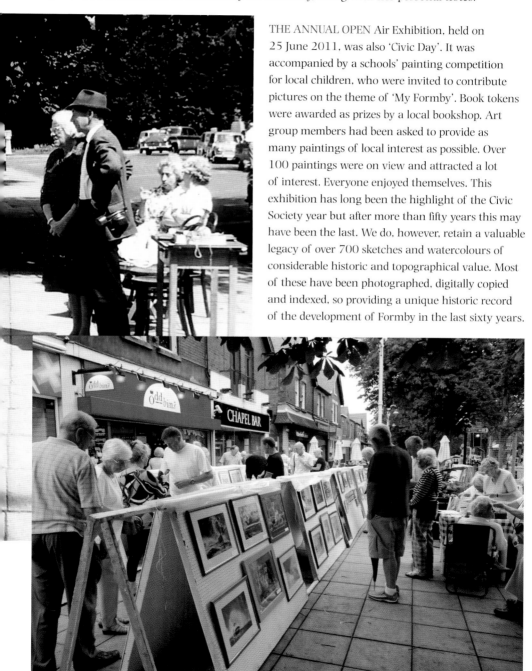

THE ANNUAL OPEN Air Exhibition, held on 25 June 2011, was also 'Civic Day'. It was accompanied by a schools' painting competition for local children, who were invited to contribute pictures on the theme of 'My Formby'. Book tokens were awarded as prizes by a local bookshop. Art group members had been asked to provide as many paintings of local interest as possible. Over 100 paintings were on view and attracted a lot of interest. Everyone enjoyed themselves. This exhibition has long been the highlight of the Civic Society year but after more than fifty years this may have been the last. We do, however, retain a valuable legacy of over 700 sketches and watercolours of considerable historic and topographical value. Most of these have been photographed, digitally copied and indexed, so providing a unique historic record of the development of Formby in the last sixty years.

If you enjoyed this book, you may also be interested in…

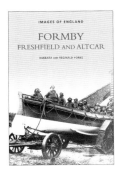

Formby, Freshfield & Altcar

REG AND BARBARA YORKE

This collection provides a pictorial record of the last century of Formby's existence. In addition to the 'traditional' picture-postcard views of the town, this intriguing selection of archive photographs portrays the everyday life, work and leisure of Formby's inhabitants. Not surprisingly, the sea has played a significant role and this is recognised by a chapter devoted to the marine rescue services. The importance of Freshfield sands in pioneer aviation and of the coastal defences in two world wars is also not forgotten.

978 0 7524 1181 1

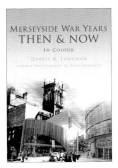

Merseyside War Years Then & Now

DANIEL K. LONGMAN

With its strategic shipping ports and factories, the towns and cities dotted along the River Mersey soon became some of Hitler's most heavily targeted sites during the Second World War. *Merseyside War Years: Then & Now* sensitively documents the changes and developments that have taken place in Merseyside since those dark days of war, demonstrating both architectural progress and Britain's resilience in the face of adversity.

978 0 7524 6352 0

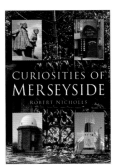

Curiosities of Merseyside

ROBERT NICHOLLS

With over 200 illustrations, Robert Nicholls has compiled a comprehensively illustrated guide to all that is remarkable or curious in Merseyside. Whether it be unusual buildings, natural features or just places associated with a fascinating story, these pages reveal an area abounding in interest. More than 140 curiosities can be found within these pages. This book will guide the reader to a wonderful range of interesting places to explore by car, public transport or on foot.

978 0 7509 3984 3

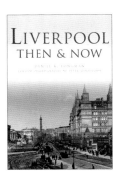

Liverpool Then & Now

DANIEL K. LONGMAN

Liverpool has a rich heritage, which is uniquely reflected in this fascinating new compilation. As well as delighting many tourists who visit this city, *Liverpool Then & Now* will provide present occupants with a glimpse of how the city used to be, in addition to awakening nostalgic memories for those who used to live or work here.

978 0 7524 5740 6

Visit our website and discover thousands of other History Press books.

www.thehistorypress.co.uk